How to Divorce Your Controlling, Manipulative, Narcissistic Husband

CHRISTOPHER R. BRUCE

HOW TO DIVORCE YOUR CONTROLLING, MANIPULATIVE, NARCISSISTIC HUSBAND
Copyright © 2017 by Christopher R. Bruce
All rights reserved.

This book or any portion thereof may not be reproduced or used in any manner whatsoever without the express written permission of the author except for the use of brief quotations in a book review.

Printed in the United States of America
First Printing, 2017

ISBN: 978-0-9975316-3-3

Christopher R. Bruce
1601 Forum Place
Suite 1101
West Palm Beach, Florida 33401
www.BrucePA.com

ACKNOWLEDGEMENTS

Thank you to my parents, Russell and Krisanne, and my wife, Ashley. Your continued love, guidance, and encouragement makes me the world's luckiest husband and son and has put me in the position of accomplishing anything I set my mind to achieving.

Thank you also to everyone who has assisted me and mentored me in the legal profession and in life. Especially to my former law partner Matthew Nugent, who for reasons I still cannot figure out, initially hired me in the middle of the worst economic downturn in recent history and gave me the opportunity to learn how to be an effective divorce litigator.

LEGAL DISCLAIMER

This book is about divorce planning and strategy and is not a legal treatise or dictionary. There are many lawyers, books and seminars which do an outstanding job explaining the numerous important intricacies of your state or country's divorce laws. My advice is to hire a competent and ethical divorce lawyer to help you understand how the laws of your state or country apply to your specific situation and to help refine the goals and strategies I tell you to implement in this book. The explanations about divorce law and strategy in this book are not a substitute for hiring a competent divorce lawyer, which is what I recommend you do.

TABLE OF CONTENTS

INTRODUCTION i
- Other Resources Designed to Help You iv
- Identify the Predator 1
- Realize You Have the Power to Change 6
- Define The Life You Want (Your Vision) 11
- Get Realistic About How Your Husband Will Act During the Divorce 14
- Keep Quiet: Don't Let Him Know What You're Planning 17
- Get Organized for Divorce 19
- Plan Your Getaway 22
- Find the Right Lawyer 25
- "Boundary Testing" 29
- Get Moving: Your Next Steps 31

Our Other Books Designed to Help You 39

ABOUT THE AUTHOR 41

INTRODUCTION

I am a divorce lawyer. You'd probably be surprised to know that, despite my profession, I am not personally a fan of divorce and everything that comes with it. For this reason, I created the website www.StayMarriedFlorida.com to help people avoid divorce (more on that soon). That said, I believe there is a time and a place for divorce. For some people, the only way to live a happy, healthy and productive life is to end their marriage. These are the people I help in my law practice.

Over the years, I've come to realize that my favorite clients to work with are women who have made the decision to divorce a controlling, manipulative, and/or narcissistic husband. In my experience, these women are not considering divorce due to a desire for money or lust; all they really seek is the right to be happy; to "be their own person"; and to avoid the sometimes every-day experience of being devalued despite their efforts to be a caring partner, parent, and person.

I am passionate about representing women looking to move on from controlling, manipulative, and/or narcissistic husbands because I know these clients are going to have a much better life when their divorce is over. I know by getting divorced, I'm helping my client get through the first stage of what can be a dramatic and positive life transformation. There is something to be said for feeling like you are making a difference in people's lives. For me, working with women seeking to leave emotionally unhealthy relationships gives me "a purpose" and "a sense of meaning" and allows me to really enjoy owning a law practice that is limited to the "uplifting" subject of handling what are often high conflict divorce and child custody disputes.

What follows in this book is a big picture overview of how you should approach everything leading up to a divorce from a controlling, manipulative, or narcissistic husband. Understanding the concepts in this book is critical, because, unfortunately, your divorce is likely going to be more complex than the typical divorce due to the personality profile of your husband.

The typical controlling narcissist-type husband is usually very intelligent, obsessed with money, and obsessed with "winning." They are often secretive about their finances, which in many cases, can be a convoluted mess. These types of men are slow to compromise, and they usually have such a charming disposition that they make for a great witness in court (and keep most people from understanding how bad it can be at times to be married to them).

While your divorce might not be hassle free, hardly anything great or important comes easy. The good news is that there are some basic things you can learn to minimize your husband's ability to make the divorce process harder than it needs to be, and these are the concepts we focus on in this book.

Divorce is not always easy, or comfortable, but it is much better when the optimal processes are de-mystified and understood. I hope this book helps you feel more confident in your situation and I wish you the best as you continue to educate yourself about the divorce process.

Christopher R. Bruce
West Palm Beach, Florida

Other Resources Designed to Help You

Before we go any further, I wanted to make a quick mention of resources I've put online to further help you navigate the divorce process, especially as the focus of this book is so narrow.

My law firm's website, **www.BrucePA.com**, has complementary books, seminars, and forums on divorce strategy, law, and procedure. Also, there are several books available for free download at www.DivorceInformationBooks.com. These books are free and include the Women's Guide for Getting Organized for Divorce, our Florida Divorce Law Guide, our guide on How to Find & Hire Your Divorce Lawyer, and Control Your Difficult Divorce, our comprehensive divorce strategy guide.

Also, because it is our belief that the real best divorce is the divorce that didn't have to happen, the Bruce Law Firm developed and supports www.StayMarriedFlorida.com, a website devoted to helping couples build, have, and keep healthy relationships. The website has articles, podcast interviews, and a growing directory of extremely talented results-driven therapists.

CHRISTOPHER R. BRUCE
HOW TO DIVORCE YOUR CONTROLLING, MANIPULATIVE, NARCISSISTIC HUSBAND

Identify the Predator

Your first step is to identify the predator. And what I mean by this is that you need to understand who your husband really is, or very well might be.

In my experience, more often than not, husbands who are controlling and manipulative have some form of a personality disorder. In many cases, these men demonstrate at least some signs of what is called narcissistic personality disorder.

Many women who have made it to the stage of reading this book are working with a therapist and have learned all about narcissism. If this term is new to you than you should consider reading up on the subject. When you google terms like "narcissist husbands" and "gaslighting" you'll probably be shocked to see how other people's stories are almost exactly describing what you have long dealt with in your own relationship.

In case you're not aware, the non-technical definition of Narcissistic Personality Disorder (according, at least, to Wikipedia) is: "*Narcissistic personality disorder is found more commonly in men. The cause is unknown…Symptoms include an excessive need for admiration,*

CHRISTOPHER R. BRUCE
HOW TO DIVORCE YOUR CONTROLLING, MANIPULATIVE, NARCISSISTIC HUSBAND

disregard for others' feelings, an inability to handle any criticism, and a sense of entitlement."

Sound familiar? I thought it might.

From my experience in hearing my client's stories, you might be dealing with a narcissistic husband if you identify with any of the following statements:

- Your husband often makes promises to you on important issues only to break them;
- Your husband puts you down in front of other people, including children and family;
- Your husband seems not to care about your feelings or hurting you;
- When you suggest marriage counseling or things to fix your relationship your husband tells you that you are the one who needs fixing;
- Your husband isolates you from others, including your family and friends;
- Your husband gets upset with you and sometimes very angry for what seem like trivial reasons, which leaves you often feeling off balance;

CHRISTOPHER R. BRUCE
HOW TO DIVORCE YOUR CONTROLLING, MANIPULATIVE, NARCISSISTIC HUSBAND

- Your husband often accuses you of not being a better wife or more attentive to his sexual needs;
- Your husband is obsessed with money and (in some cases) keeps details of finances shielded from you;
- Your husband makes threats on what will happen to you if you leave him or "rules by threats" in the relationship; or
- Your husband accuses you of being unfaithful but he is a serial cheater.

Also, other common traits I commonly, but not always find associated with narcissistic husbands are:

- Your husband is an only child (or only male child) and has an extremely controlling mother;
- You had a very quick courtship/engagement before getting married or your husband began dating you while he was married to another woman and told you terrible things about the previous wife (some of which you now know or suspect were not true); or
- Your husband is a doctor or engineer.

The point of this chapter is not to give you a degree in psychology but you have to understand who it really is that you are dealing with. This is because people with narcissistic personality disorders or those who are habitually controlling and manipulative *will almost never be capable of changing who they are*. No matter how hard you try to please him, no matter how much love you give, no matter how hard you try to change, he is likely never going to become the husband you want him to be. In fact, sadly, with age, he will probably just get worse.

I have had some many very wonderful women in my office who cannot get themselves to accept the reality of who their husband is, and how he is never going to change. Don't let this be you. You don't have to get divorced and I'm not trying to encourage you to do so. The reason you need to accept the fact of who your husband is and how he will likely change is because if you don't you are just going to repeatedly make yourself upset by trying and failing to fix the situation. That's the sad reality.

If you know your husband has a personality disorder (or think he might have one after reading this) than you should strongly consider working with an experienced therapist for the sole purpose of helping you develop and implement strategies for accepting who your husband is, learning that you and your future is not defined by who your husband is and how he has treated you, and having the confidence to move on from your husband if that is what you determine, after careful consideration, is necessary for you to have the happy and fulfilling life that you yearn to be living.

If you don't know any therapists, ask around for referrals or check out therapists listed on our website, www.StayMarriedFlorida.com. If you cannot find an therapist in your area please reach out to my law firm and we will help you get the appropriate referral.

Realize You Have the Power to Change

Over the years of being a divorce lawyer, my clients have given me every reason under the sun to justify to me why they want a divorce. Some tell me they need divorce because their spouse ignores them or their relationship is not much different than two ships passing in the night. Others say their spouse smothers them, making it impossible for them to be their own person. In the morning, I'll hear a husband tell me about how he wants out of the marriage because his wife sits at home all day refusing to get a "real job" and in the afternoon, another will tell me divorce is the only answer because his wife is a workaholic who neglects the family, or doesn't want to have a family. Housewives tell me how they suspect an affair because their husband is ignoring them sexually while others complain their spouse is a sex addict.

Sometimes, I feel like I've heard it all when it comes to reasons for a breakdown of a marriage but I sleep soundly at night knowing there is always a new story out there for me to hear.

CHRISTOPHER R. BRUCE
HOW TO DIVORCE YOUR CONTROLLING, MANIPULATIVE, NARCISSISTIC HUSBAND

The funny thing about human nature is seldom do people to initially realize their role in problem creation. It is a rare day that a person tells me in a client interview how their arrival in my office was the culmination of their own personal, misguided decision-making over the preceding years or decades. Many people, understandably, blame the other person for the divorce, and are resistant to admitting their role in creating an unhappy marriage.

Is your life currently miserable? Do you feel like your spouse is stealing your happiness; sealing you off from the world; continuously putting you down; polluting your children or grandchildren; fracturing your family; or injecting toxicity into a relationship in ways you never thought possible? Guess what? **<u>You are part of the problem</u>**.

You might not like hearing this, but you are better off realizing reality now. Your life decisions are a great part of why you are in a marriage you think needs to end. Your choices led you to where you are right now. Believe it or not, if you are unhappy, miserable, beaten down, or [insert other description of your life] part of the reason is because *you did it to yourself.*

Before you throw this book or your reading device at the wall and take to vilifying me for being insensitive, chauvinistic, or inhuman, do yourself a favor and read the rest of this chapter. It will make your life better. I promise.

You are not to blame for your husband's unfair and abusive behavior. You should not feel like you created your husband's controlling behavior, inability to appreciate you, chronic addictions, or serial philandering. I especially stress towards the women reading this book who have been in long-term abusive relationships that they should not feel like they are responsible for making their husband into who he is now and now feel responsible to stay with him.

My point in telling you that "you did it to yourself" is to help you realize that you created the situation of being in a relationship that you are contemplating leaving (or maybe deep down wanting to fix). Rarely anyone in this day and age, in the western world, can say they were actually forced to get married. The bottom line is this: part of what led you to where you are today, a life you are not happy with, was a series of conscious decisions made by you. So, that's why you need to realize that *you are part of the problem*. Part of why you are here is because, *you did it to yourself*.

The good news is you also have the ability to make choices that make your life better. Just like you - likely without knowing it –

helped create your marital problems and unhappiness, you have the ability to create something better. Coming to the realization that you have the power to change your life is probably the most important thing you can do as part of the divorce process. Part of having the *Best Divorce* is learning that you have, and have always had the power to control your own destiny, and then using that knowledge to create the life you desire and deserve. This knowledge is especially empowering for those who have been beaten down over time by chronically selfish or abusive spouses.

Knowing that you, and only you, ultimately control your life going forward, helps you be in the driver's seat when it comes to the divorce process. When you overcome your doubts that you could have a better life in the future, you will be in a much better mindset when it comes to determining what it is you really want out of the divorce. Further, in future relationships, you will be less prone to the desperate decision-making that can cause you to relapse into the same problems that plagued your first marriage.

Before you go any further, take the time to develop and cope with the understanding that your life decisions helped create the situation you want to fix. Then, do your best to get over what has happened in the past. Realize that you have the absolute ability to control your path to living a happy, healthy and prosperous life. Coming to this realization and understanding, with yourself, might just be the most transforming and worthwhile moment you've ever experienced.

If you felt like this chapter was too "touchy feely" for you, or did not present any actionable advice, I'll state things differently and in a language you might understand: You helped cause this mess. Get your head out of the sand, suck it up, and stop blaming others for your problems. Your divorce will be quicker, cost less money, and you'll be better off afterwards. Get it? Got it? Good.

Define The Life You Want (Your Vision)

You need to define the life after your divorce before you spend any more time contemplating divorce. If you could push a magic button and instantly be "living the dream," what would that be like? How would your life change? Invest the time going through what I'll call the "Who, What, Where, When, Why and How of Separation and Life Improvement." Before you go any further, you absolutely must be able to answer the following questions:

- Who do you want to be as a person?

- What would it take to make you happier and healthier?

- Where would you be living and what type of people would you surround yourself with?

- Why would this life be better than your life is now?

- How is divorce a necessary part of you having this life?

Engaging in this analysis, or something like it, is critical. You must have a picture in your mind of what your favored life after the divorce will be. Otherwise, you'll lack serious direction in how you move forward, and you will not be making purpose-driven decisions when it comes to handling the legal aspects of your divorce.

I doubt you would ever consider investing half of your life savings - which is what many lose in their divorce - in a business, idea, or person, without a compelling reason. Divorce should be no different. You need to know your end game, your big picture purpose, before you begin anything. Divorce, no matter how well done, will disrupt your family, friendships, and finances. It would be a huge shame for you to endure the divorce process and not have a better life to show for it. Do yourself a favor and take the time now to understand what you want out of life when the divorce is done. Taking this step costs nothing but your time and brainpower.

If you have no idea what your life after the divorce should be, it might be a sign that you are living it already and things might not be as bad as they seem. Sometimes, people are stressed out with their job, the death of a family member, or something equally traumatic, and end up believing divorce is the answer to making their life better because it is what they've seen others doing. Don't let yourself be one of these people.

CHRISTOPHER R. BRUCE
HOW TO DIVORCE YOUR CONTROLLING, MANIPULATIVE, NARCISSISTIC HUSBAND

That said, determining what your idea life might not come easy if you have spent most of your adult years in a toxic relationship. If you are having a hard time understanding what you want your life to be, or envisioning any other life than the miserable one you are living, you need to spend some time with an experienced therapist. They will help you determine why you are unhappy and whether divorce should be part of the solution. The therapist will help you develop a vision of hope and change, even if your husband has always held you down. Your health insurance likely covers the therapy expense. Most therapists offer evening appointments to accommodate those who work long hours during the day. If you do not know a therapist, I've listed plenty of the great ones in South Florida on StayMarriedFlorida.com.

Once you develop your vision of your "ideal life" I encourage you to write it down and revisit and refine it often. Life is always a "work in progress" and your vision for your future is no different.

Get Realistic About How Your Husband Will Act During the Divorce

Once you have taken the time to get confidence in yourself to move on and developed a vision of what you want to move to, you need to "get real". By this I mean: remember who you're dealing with.

Many of my clients are women who have been in some form of an abusive relationship (always being controlled and manipulated is abuse) with their husband and they're used to seeing the best in people. That's why they've stayed with their husband as long as they have and the natural tendency of you is probably to do that.

But when you're getting divorced from somebody who has historically been controlling/manipulative, and probably has personality disorder, you've got to get real and remember who you're dealing with. Don't kid yourself. Understand the reality of what your likely narcissistic husband is going to be like during the divorce.

If your husband manipulated you or intimidated you during the marriage, he's going to be even worse during the

CHRISTOPHER R. BRUCE
HOW TO DIVORCE YOUR CONTROLLING, MANIPULATIVE, NARCISSISTIC HUSBAND

divorce. Don't believe what he tells you. Get professionals to deal with him. You're not going to be able to.

If your husband was obsessed with money before, during the marriage, he's going to be during the divorce. And will go to extremes, in some situations, to keep as much of it as possible. And you've got to understand sometimes you have to be ready if you need that money, to fight to the end to get it. Don't kid yourself, it's not going to be easy.

If your husband kept financial secrets from you during the marriage, likely he's not going to be forthcoming with you during the divorce. You're either going to need to obtain the information before the divorce starts, and more on that later, or make him realize he has no choice besides coming clean. Otherwise the reality is the attorney that you hire is going to have to take some time to get this information out of him, because being forthcoming with others on "his" finances is not something that comes natural.

If your husband is somebody who turned other disagreements with people during the marriage into personal vendettas, he's probably going to do the same thing during the divorce and it's not going to be easy for you. Which is why you have to be very careful as you set up this process.

And then to the biggest (and sad) reality. If your husband lacked the ability to care about you or others during the marriage, he's not going to wake up and do the right thing during the divorce. You're going to have to push hard and apply the right pressures to get what you need.

No, you're not doomed or destined for failure just because your husband is a difficult person. There are strategies for dealing with the problems your husband is likely going to inject into a divorce. But just don't kid yourself into thinking that when you file for divorce, your husband's going to all of a sudden be a different and better person. He won't.

Understand now that your husband's worst qualities will be magnified and become worse. And if you accept this and plan for this fact, you will be much more likely to get divorced on fair terms, sooner, because the people that are going to help you do this are going to be able to take into account these realities and come up with the appropriate legal strategies to deal with them.

CHRISTOPHER R. BRUCE
HOW TO DIVORCE YOUR CONTROLLING, MANIPULATIVE, NARCISSISTIC HUSBAND

Keep Quiet: Don't Let Him Know What You're Planning

Step five, as you think about getting divorced from a difficult or narcissistic husband is you need to understand how to keep quiet. Do not allow your husband to think that you're filing for divorce before you are locked, loaded, and ready to go.

If you tip him off to what you are planning, and he believes you, he's going to resort to all of his worst qualities and go into a defensive mode and manipulate you until the timing for divorce is right for <u>him</u>. I see this all the time and it never ends well.

When contemplating divorce from a husband like yours, it's going to be challenging enough just with dealing with him. You don't want him to have an opportunity to make the case more complicated than it needs to be by finding out from you now, before you are ready, that you're thinking about divorcing him.

Instead, you have to take the time to make the decision that divorce is the correct decision. See the therapist and do the things we've talked about so far. But otherwise keep your lips sealed. Keep quiet. Get ready, get organized, go get to a lawyer and the lawyer will handle how your husband finds out (more on all of this to come- keep reading). Don't worry, there are plenty of things for you to be doing right now but telling your husband what you are thinking about doing or planning to do is not one of them!

CHRISTOPHER R. BRUCE
HOW TO DIVORCE YOUR CONTROLLING, MANIPULATIVE, NARCISSISTIC HUSBAND

Get Organized for Divorce

Before you divorce a controlling or narcissistic husband you need to gather what you can now in terms of financial records. Get copies of as many financial documents as possible. Start making a current and after divorce budget. You're going to play the role of an investigator, and this is a little bit empowering when you don't have access to this information.

Try your best to make a list of the assets and debt that you're aware of and start trying to get an idea in your head of things that you might want to have after the divorce while being realistic.

Try your best to make a summary of your financials, at least of what you know, because you're probably not going to know or be able to know everything about your finances when you're married to a difficult and controlling person. But do your best to gather as much as you can, and try to get three years of records. Before you go see a lawyer or say anything to your husband, gather as much as you can.

We've tried to make it easy for you to understand exactly what you need to gather through our law firm's book, *A Women's*

CHRISTOPHER R. BRUCE
HOW TO DIVORCE YOUR CONTROLLING, MANIPULATIVE, NARCISSISTIC HUSBAND

Guide to Getting Organized for Divorce. You can get your free download of the book at www.GetOrganizedForDivorce.com, and in the email with the download will be an option to request the book by mail, or pickup at our law firm's office if you'd rather not have anything go in the mail.

On this note, there's a value to getting as much information up front as possible, but don't use the need to get more information or gather more bank statements as an indefinite excuse for not moving forward to fix the fact that you're married to somebody you need to get away from.

Take the time to gather as much as you can but don't let it be an excuse for delaying you from moving *from* a relationship to where you're constantly put down *to* a life to where you have the ability to finally be free, respect yourself, and enjoy each and every day.

There is a little bit involved sometimes with getting organized and my firm's book mentioned above was written specifically for women in your situation who are contemplating divorce . The book covers, in granular detail, how to gather what you need and do so in a secure manner so your husband doesn't know what's going on. The book also covers how to analyze the information you gather and how you can go from knowing nothing to being much more educated and aware of the marital finances (even if you don't consider yourself to be a "numbers person") and how things might play out in a divorce before you even go talk to a lawyer. It's a whole book just on these issues.

The website for the book is www.GetOrganizedForDivorce.com. That'll direct you right to the link for the book I've written on this, which is free by the way. All my books are free for you to download from my websites. You can even request my firm to mail them for you. Or we'll put a package together if you're afraid of getting mail so you can come pick it up at an office location. Our thought is educated consumers and educated wives will make the right decisions for themselves. And we do that as a service to our community. We want to get the information out there.

In terms of marital information for you, you need to gather what you can, as much as possible. Take the time to do that. It will help you and any lawyer that you hire a great deal and allow the fact that you might have a difficult divorce to be a difficult but shorter divorce. It's critical.

CHRISTOPHER R. BRUCE
HOW TO DIVORCE YOUR CONTROLLING, MANIPULATIVE, NARCISSISTIC HUSBAND

Plan Your Getaway

Step seven, when you're divorcing a narcissistic or controlling husband, is to start thinking about where you can go and how you can fund your "getaway".

If finances allow, and that's "the big if", it's best to get out of the house when you are filing for divorce. Because, when you're around somebody like your husband, if he's a controlling person, his natural tendency will be to try to manipulate you and do things that make it very, very difficult for you to have the fortitude to get through the divorce and get the settlement that you should have under the law (and need for your future). If you are in the same house with your husband during the divorce he is going to have a much easier time filling your head with the types of threats and other nonsense that my clients come to my office crying about and can oftentimes tempt even strong women to "take a bad deal" in the divorce just so it is over.

If finances allow it, and that's the big if, I'd prefer that my clients be out of the house living somewhere else or with relatives. Maybe if there's a second home, stay in the second home. Just get into a place where you don't have to listen to your husband every night as the divorce is carrying out.

You're also going to need to think of ways you can get the money you need, in the short term, to pay for those living expenses and your legal expenses. And this might mean securing commitments for help from others in your family or identifying assets that you have that you can strategically transfer into your control so that you can pay for your short term living expenses and to hire a lawyer.

Many of the good lawyers will, ultimately, look to your husband to get paid, but they're going to be requiring you to pay money up front to them to get started to cover the first several months of work that it can take to depose your husband and get into court if a case is not settled. Usually it can take $15,000-25,000 to do what is necessary to depose your husband and do everything that is necessary to get the type of court hearing needed to make him pay your lawyer for continued litigation.

The exact cost of the lawyer will vary (and you usually get what you pay for) but the one thing that is constant is you are going to need to think about now is how you might go about getting the money you need to live independently for the short term and pay your lawyer to get started.

It may be the case that that money is just not there. And if that is the case, "it is what it is" and it will just have to be dealt with and that's one of the things you're going to want to talk to a lawyer about.

Ultimately, your lawyer will help you come up with the best strategy tailored to your specific situation. There is no "cookie cutter" divorce from a difficult and controlling husband. That said, generally, I'll tell you that when my clients come to me and they have the ability to find financial resources that allow them to get away from their husband, at least for the short term, right as the divorce is being filed until things settle down, I usually have them do it.

CHRISTOPHER R. BRUCE
HOW TO DIVORCE YOUR CONTROLLING, MANIPULATIVE, NARCISSISTIC HUSBAND

Find the Right Lawyer

Step eight in this process is to find the right lawyer. The bottom line when divorcing a narcissistic type husband who has a history of intimidating or controlling you is you need to get a lawyer or you're going to get railroaded.

Don't try to be cheap and think that you're going to deal with this yourself. Most people do not need lawyers to get divorced but you do because this is just one of those situations to where you're not going to be in an equal bargaining position without one.

Go find an honest attorney who understands how to deal with someone like your husband. There are plenty of honest divorce lawyers. There are a lot of screw-balls in my field, but there are also a lot of really good, professional people who make a career out of helping you through this situation the right way. You need to go find one of these people because otherwise it is not going to end well for you.

If you have trouble being on an equal playing field with your husband in day to day affairs during your marriage, it's going to be even worse during the divorce. You're not going to be negotiating with a person who you're afraid of and coming out on the winning end. That is just the bottom line. And to find the right lawyer for your situation, talk around, talk to your therapist. If you don't know a therapist, talk to the attorneys that you do know or trusted friends who've experienced divorce from a difficult person. And you want to have a lawyer who only handles divorce cases and has a track record of taking difficult divorce cases to court.

You can have any type of divorce lawyer, but my suggestion is you need someone who is very comfortable going to court. Find somebody who handles high conflict divorce cases and is not afraid to take a case to trial. When you have somebody like your husband who's controlling and manipulative to you, often times you have to have what's a little bit more of an aggressive legal strategy and not a lawyer who is counting on your husband to rise to the occasion and "do the right thing". Such an approach works in many divorces but will not in yours.

The attorney has to be confident in their ability to try a case or advance a case to deal with uncomfortable situations and move your case forward. They have to understand the type of person that your husband is. If your husband determines your lawyer is conflict adverse than he will start to run circles around your attorney and use making your lawyer uncomfortable as a means to try and get your own attorney to influence you into making poor settlement decisions.

A husband who is controlling, manipulative, and/or a narcissist is not somebody who you can negotiate with in good faith. Often dealing with them requires a strategic (sometimes subtle) showing of force. Your husband is going to have to respect the person that you hired. If they think your lawyer does not have a backbone than they're just going to treat your lawyer how they treat you. And look where that got you. You've got to have a lawyer who knows what they're doing or it is going to be a bad situation for you.

I put out a book on how to evaluate and hire divorce lawyers. While of course I'd love for you to consider my law firm, there are other really outstanding lawyers in the community and the best thing for you to do is interview a few lawyers and find the right fit. If you are like most women I represent, you probably have not spent a lot of time in the past interviewing attorneys, so this might be a bit intimidating. Don't let this be the case. Go to www.AllAboutDivorceLawyers.com and you'll be able to get our firm's free book on *How to Find, Hire, and Worth With Your Divorce Lawyer* so that you can take this step with confidence.

CHRISTOPHER R. BRUCE
HOW TO DIVORCE YOUR CONTROLLING, MANIPULATIVE, NARCISSISTIC HUSBAND

"Boundary Testing"

Step nine, and we've got ten steps so we're almost done here. What we are covering now is helping you beware of something called "boundary testing" so you can start practicing independence now.

Your husband, in the divorce, is likely going to start "boundary testing" as soon as the divorce starts. This means that he will, very early on, try to see how capable he's going to be in controlling you and your lawyer. The key on how to handle these behaviors during the divorce is to *"be assertive but do not be a jerk."*

If you let your husband see that he can continue to control you or worse yet, control your lawyer, then you're going to be up a creek. This can be hard to prevent when he's historically manipulated or controlled you (which is why I suggest you try to live somewhere where he cannot constantly badger you during the divorce). Basically, what needs to happen here is you need to "retrain the dog" when the divorce starts. By this I mean show your husband that during the divorce, he's not going to control you anymore.

CHRISTOPHER R. BRUCE
HOW TO DIVORCE YOUR CONTROLLING, MANIPULATIVE, NARCISSISTIC HUSBAND

I know- easier said than done. You can start practicing for this, taking steps every day, to let your husband know he's not going to control you anymore. This doesn't require confrontation, it can be as simple as you not following his rules (or some of his rules) anymore. Practice makes perfect here. It's not going to be natural to you at first.

Your husband may not give you credit for becoming more independent and may blame your lawyer or someone else for the change in how you act. But my thought is: who cares? You're going to feel better, you're going to feel like you're not being controlled. You're going to feel like, day by day, you are a step closer to the life that you really want to be living. This type of progress can be contagious, so watch out!

In all seriousness, understand that boundary testing will be an issue during the divorce and when you can, consider starting taking little steps now to stand up for yourself when your husband tries to control you. If you don't have a therapist already, consider getting one for purposes of helping you on this point. If you don't know any therapists, take a look at those who are listed on www.StayMarriedFlorida.com or call my office and we'll reach out to our network and find you several qualified people to consider.

Get Moving: Your Next Steps

What you need to do now is get moving towards a life that you want to be proud about. Getting results requires *taking action*.

Yes, knowledge is power. It is important to educate yourself on strategies to deal with your husband and what will happen during the divorce. But you have to be careful. Don't perpetually delay your need to make your life better out of perceived need to learn more or gather more information.

The mind is a powerful thing and odds are, deep down, you're afraid of moving forward. Be cognizant of the fact that sometimes you may find yourself trying to learn more, gather more, do more before you take action. Remember that getting results requires *taking action*.

Next Steps:

So a couple of next action steps, as least as recommended by a divorce lawyer… Before you do anything else, if you haven't yet, you need to go see a therapist who really knows what they're doing. I've got a plenty of great ones listed at www.StayMarriedFlorida.com. These are amazing therapists, most of which I've seen care a lot about my clients, that I trust completely. They're on my website, there's a lot of other great ones. If you haven't seen a therapist yet, you need to. This is not necessarily for marriage counseling. It's for helping you evaluate your situation, the relationship with your husband, and things that you can do to try to make it better if you have not.

If you've made the decision or are thinking of making the decision to move on from your husband, these therapists are critical. Therapists are basically a partner or coach in you transitioning to the life that you really want. It's a very hard thing to do without professional help; these people make a living out of helping you get from where you are now to a happier life and help you be as comfortable and confident in yourself during the process, as possible. They can also give you strategies for dealing with a difficult spouse and day to day life and during a period of transition and conflict, like divorce cam sometimes can be.

In case you are wondering, I am not by my nature a *"huggy-feel good, California leftist, had my own therapist since birth"* type of person. I'm a weekend redneck. I put on my suit when I meet with you or go to court but that's about it. I refuse to do the lawyer thing and drive one of those fast little foreign cars because I drive a pickup truck that can run them all over- and the only thing that could change is that I'll buy a bigger truck. Heck, early in my practice I thought therapy was just a bunch of "kumbaya" nonsense. But, with all this said, when I devoted myself to mastering my area of the law, I learned, time and time again, how important it is for people in crisis or people who are going through a period of life transition such as a divorce from a difficult person, to work with a therapist. If you are adverse to therapy, think of the therapist as a consult or a coach, because consulting or coaching on a very narrow set of issues is really what the therapist is doing for you.

So, before you do anything, go see a really good therapist. Otherwise, it's going to be impossible for you, more likely than not, to get the results you need in the divorce with a lawyer, even if you have the best lawyer in the world. If your head's not on straight for this, if you're not prepared, if you don't have the right mindset, the divorce is going to be very, very, very difficult, just like your husband.

Otherwise, as far as follow up items, I've got five of them for you.

CHRISTOPHER R. BRUCE
HOW TO DIVORCE YOUR CONTROLLING, MANIPULATIVE, NARCISSISTIC HUSBAND

Follow Up Step #1: Define Your Ideal Life & Develop Your Divorce Strategy

The first thing you need to do is start to envision and define your own life and develop a strategy for your divorce. We're just talking big picture to start. I've got a whole book on the best ways, strategically, to approach a divorce with things to be aware of, how your lawyer should be litigating the case, what to do before you even make mention of divorce or even go see a lawyer or even gather your first documents. There's a lot of stuff that you should be thinking about to really do this in the correct way possible.

The book on this for you to read is *Control Your Difficult Divorce*, and you can download a free copy at www.ControlYourDifficultDivorce.com. It's a free download and after you sign up for the download you'll get an email giving you the ability to request a copy of the book by mail too. The book covers both how to develop the right mindset for divorce, and then how to develop and implement a legal strategy designed to control a difficult person (like your husband) to get a fair result as soon as possible.

Step #2: Learn the Basics of the Law

Another thing that's important to do that has not been discussed at all really in this book is to learn the basics of the laws that will apply in your divorce, and understand what's going to happen and when it's going to happen in your divorce.

And guess what; we've got a book on that too, and also a video. You can request your book at www.FloridaDivorceLawGuide.com and you can watch a one hour overview video on the website at www.BrucePa.com/FloridaDivorceLawGuide. Read the books and watch the videos. In an hour an a half you'll learn what you need to learn. Just understand the basics now; a lawyer will fill you in on the rest.

Step #3: Get Organized

Next you need to start getting organized, gathering your financial information and figuring out what you want in your divorce, to the extent you can figure it out. Go check out my book for women, *A Women's Guide to Getting Organized for Divorce*. It really tells you everything you need to know. It's a quick, easy read. www.GetOrganizedForDivorce.com. Do not skip this step; getting organized for divorce is one of the most important steps you're going to take.

Step #4: Start Meeting Lawyers

After you are organized, start interviewing divorce lawyers, even if you are not yet ready to start the divorce. Get to the point where you have picked a lawyer to work with when and if the timing is right for you pursue divorce.

Oftentimes these meetings with attorneys can be very, very helpful because they're going to dispel a lot of the common myths about divorce with your situation. They're probably going to help put you at ease with a lot of your worries and until you go and hear the answers from somebody who does this stuff for a living every day and is good at it, there's going to be a lot of worry. Oftentimes worry is caused by the unknown. Once you have a better idea of what's going to happen in your divorce and the best way to approach it, you're going to feel much more comfortable and at ease.

Many of my clients will have initially have a meeting with me. I call the meetings a consultation and strategy session. Usually the meeting is about one and a half, two hours. My team and I take the time before the meeting to gather background information from you, so that I can understand your situation and your most pressing questions before we meet. Then, during the meeting, I address all of your concerns, how the law applies to your situation, and leave you with a plan of action to follow when and if you are ready to move forward. We'll offer to record the conversation upon request, so that you can have to reference back to later. What I do in these initial meetings costs "a couple of bucks" but -*in my completely biased opinion*- it's worth it to have more certainty in what will likely happen and what needs to happen if you pursue divorce, and in many cases the people who know what they're doing in my field often do not give "free consultations" because if they did they'd spend all day giving them.

People who meet with me may not hire me for another year, or ever, but it allows them a better idea of what might happen in a divorce, which is important so when their husband is threatening them about "what happens if they leave", they know what is and isn't true.

Step #5: Move Forward

Step five is file for divorce with your lawyer. The sooner you start the process, the sooner you'll start to feel better and the sooner this will be done. For many of you, the hardest part about the entire divorce process is going to be actually starting it. After that, the theory is that you hire the right people and they deal with everything while you keep moving on towards the life you want to be living for yourself. It may not be the case that your divorce, from a legal perspective, is extremely complicated. It's just that you're divorcing a difficult person. And the sooner you start that, the sooner you get it done.

I will say this: you cannot get divorced until you're ready. Only you know when it's right for you. Don't take any of this book as me encouraging you to go file for divorce. There's enough divorces going on to keep my firm and all the others in business.

Just recognize that the sooner you start, the sooner it's over. It may not be a simple process or quick, but the sooner the divorce is behind you, the quicker you're going to be living the life you that you deserve. Quite frankly, to be living a life that you can be proud about.

Our Other Books Designed to Help You

Hopefully you have found this book helpful to you in your time of need. This book was very narrowly focused and does not even begin to touch on many of the other questions that might be in your head about divorce and everything that comes with it. In case you were looking to learn more, I wanted to make sure you knew that this is not the Bruce Law Firm's only book.

The Bruce Law Firm has several books available for free download at www.DivorceInformationBooks.com. These books are free and include this Florida Divorce Law Guide, the Women's Guide to Getting Organized for Divorce, our guide on How to Find, Hire, & Work With Your Divorce Lawyer, and Control Your Difficult Divorce, our comprehensive divorce strategy guide.

Also, because it is our belief that the real best divorce is the divorce that didn't have to happen, the Bruce Law Firm developed and supports www.StayMarriedFlorida.com, a website devoted to helping couples build, have, and keep healthy relationships. The

CHRISTOPHER R. BRUCE
HOW TO DIVORCE YOUR CONTROLLING, MANIPULATIVE, NARCISSISTIC HUSBAND

website has articles, podcast interviews, and a growing directory of extremely talented results-driven therapists.

If you found this free book helpful, the best compliment you could give would be to share our books with others who might be in need (just direct them to www.DivorceInformationBooks.com). Also, we love it when people spread the word about the Bruce Law Firm on Avvo.com (google Christopher R. Bruce Avvo and click to leave a review) or our google business page (google Bruce Law Firm West Palm Beach and click the link to leave a google review).

ABOUT THE AUTHOR

Christopher R. Bruce is a divorce lawyer and appellate lawyer for divorce cases and has been for nearly all of his legal career. His law practice is predominately limited to representing his South Florida clients in divorce and family court matters involving business valuation and asset tracing issues, the need to confront a difficult or intimidating person, the prosecution or defense of long term financial support claims, or serious issues involving children.

Chris takes a particular interest in representing women in divorces from narcissistic or emotionally abusive/manipulative husbands. This is because Chris feels these cases are most likely to result in his client having a dramatically improved and transformed-for-the-better life once the divorce is over.

Chris founded the Bruce Law Firm, P.A. in November 2016. Previously, he enjoyed the pleasure of practicing for seven and a half years with divorce lawyers Matthew S. Nugent and Adam M. Zborowski. Their law partnership, Nugent Zborowski & Bruce, was located in North Palm Beach, Florida, and was limited to representing clients in divorce and child custody cases.

Chris is a native of Palm Beach County, Florida, and a graduate of Palm Beach Gardens High School. Outside of the office, and spending time with his family, his passion is saltwater fishing and marine conservation. Chris enjoys participating in South Florida billfish tournaments and promoting marine species and habitat conservation.

Chris frequently publishes articles on current topics in Florida Divorce Law, and serves as a resource to news agencies reporting on Florida divorce issues. His articles have appeared in the *South Florida Daily Business Review*, *Palm Beach County Bar Bulletin* and several other Florida Bar publications. A proponent of keeping families together, Chris developed www.StayMarriedFlorida.com, a resource for helping people build, have, and keep happy and healthy relationships.

Chris developed www.BrucePA.com to further help people create the best probability for making their divorce a *"Best Divorce"* that allows them to move on to a life to be proud about when their divorce is over. The website's resources include complementary books, seminars, and forums on divorce strategy, law, and procedure.

If you would like to contact Chris in regards to a Florida divorce or family law matter, this book, or anything else, you can call (561) 810-0170 or go to **www.BrucePA.com.**

Made in the USA
Columbia, SC
20 September 2019